Everyone is all atwitter about *Tweet Land of Liberty*

"Devilishly and deliciously witty. We could all use a laugh a day, and Elinor Lipman has given me that."
—JUDY BLUME

"It's nice to see that Lipman's wit has escaped the hell of Twitter and collected itself in a book."
—JONATHAN FRANZEN

"A devotion of fearless, sassy, sublime insights that should be carried into the voting booth of our daily lives—each poem read again and again—before any lever is pulled."
—NIKKY FINNEY

"Wise and sassy and too fun to miss!"
—JILL MCCORKLE

"This year, has there been any better way to revel in the political process than to pour a cup of coffee, log on to Twitter, and read one of Elinor Lipman's clever, catchy tweets about the race for the presidency? With humor, wit, and no small share of brilliance, Lipman has cataloged the 2012 election in delectable sound bytes that manage to capture what we're all secretly thinking—in rhyme, and in less than 140 characters."
—JODI PICOULT

"Jon Stewart in 140 characters. What could be better?"
—STACY SCHIFF

"Winsome, witty, and winning! I don't know how she does it!!"
—ANITA SHREVE

"Elinor Lipman tweets like a nightingale with an eagle eye."
—CATHLEEN SCHINE

"Dorothy Parker, Ogden Nash, Calvin Trillin, and Elinor Lipman!!"
—MAMEVE MEDWED

"If brevity be / The soul of wit / Then Elinor has / A surefire hit."
.—ALEX BEAM

"Elinor Lipman is to tweets what Shakespeare is to sonnets."
—FIROOZEH DUMAS

"There once was a Lipman on Twitter, who made every liberal titter."
—MICHAEL LOWENTHAL

"I'm beset with Lipmania."
—HENRY ALFORD

"So it has come to this! Of thee I zing. I love it."
—LOIS LOWRY

"The only sane, smart, and witty thing to come out of the Republican primaries."
—STEPHEN MCCAULEY

"First I laughed my way through Elinor Lipman's book of political tweets. Then I put my ear to the ground and listened to Molly Ivins guffawing from the grave. Lipman is a piquant poetic rock star!"
—WALLY LAMB

Tweet Land
of
Liberty

Tweet Land

of

Liberty

Irreverent Rhymes from
the Political Circus

Elinor Lipman

BEACON PRESS, BOSTON

BEACON PRESS
25 Beacon Street
Boston, Massachusetts 02108-2892
www.beacon.org; @beaconpress

Beacon Press books
are published under the auspices of
the Unitarian Universalist Association of Congregations.

15 14 13 12   8 7 6 5 4 3 2 1

This book is printed on acid-free paper that meets the
uncoated paper ANSI/NISO specifications for permanence
as revised in 1992.

Text design by Kim Arney

Library of Congress Cataloging-in-Publication Data

Lipman, Elinor.
   Tweet land of liberty : irreverent rhymes from the political
circus / Elinor Lipman.
      p.   cm.
   ISBN 978-0-8070-4243-4 (paperback : alk. paper)
1. Presidents—United States—Election—2012—Poetry.
2. Political candidates—United States—Poetry.
3. Humorous poetry, American.   I. Title.
   PS3562.I577T94 2012
   811'.54—dc22   2012021292

I place this name in nomination,
A deeply grateful dedication:
For Beacon's Atwan, without you,
My tweets were only *temps perdu*.

A Note from the Poet

I apologize. Like you, I thought Twitter was for movie stars, egomaniacs, and nobodies in need of giving their inner musings a megaphone. Then I went to a social networking lecture in June of 2011—not because I was interested but because the panelists were friends and I wanted to be collegial. They were all believers and cited many examples of Twitter stars with hundreds of thousands of followers, cult-like.

"You'd be good at it," one said to me on the way out. She mentioned "cleverness" and "a way with words." And true to what an editor once confided ("An author never forgets a compliment"), I said I'd sign up/sign on—whatever one did.

I posted my first tweet a few days later, coincident with Governor Andrew Cuomo's announcing the passage of New York's same-sex marriage bill. That was good; it didn't reference me, my novels, or the chicken I was fricasseeing. I told my son I was Twittering. "*Tweeting*, Ma," he corrected. Soon I had two followers.

The next morning, at my kitchen table, I thought: Political tweets in rhyme? I had bona fides, didn't I? I'd had a long rhyming faux valentine "from" Bill to Hillary Clinton published in *Huffington Post* and a rhyming homage to Michelle Obama's clothes that appeared on a website devoted to exactly that topic. I'd been obsessed with presidential politics since my early intense crush on John F. Kennedy, and I had published a series of blowhard op-ed pieces in the *Boston Globe* in '08. So without enough self-reflection, I pledged on Facebook and Twitter to post one political tweet a day until the election. I should've counted how far away November 6, 2012, was (499 days), and I should've promised only a five-day week. But a pledge is a pledge. I used Yom Kippur 2011 as an excuse to take one day off and am desperately looking forward to Yom Kippur 2012.

Did I have a goal, other than entertaining my fellow political junkies? A book would be nice, I thought. I asked the editor of my novels, who murmured something about shelf life and putting all her energy into my fiction. I did not, in bookselling parlance, go out with it. Facebook friends often wrote under my daily poems, "Book book book." I wrote back, "Don't think so, unless it's construction paper and yarn."

Then this storybook thing happened: In Boston, not long ago, in the middle of a very loud party, Beacon Press's publisher and editorial director (translation: *can make a book deal all by herself*) said, "Someone's doing your tweets as a book, right?"

I said "Why, no."

"Well, *I* am," she said. And exactly four months later, this preemie is born.

Actually, I love writing these. I love rhyming, that out-of-fashion art form. I am proud to have met syllabic challenges like "Blagojevich," "Callista," "Tiffany's," and to have rhymed "Santorum" in a believable context with "Purim." I even like the 140-character limit that Twitter imposes. It's easier for me now than it was at the beginning. I tell myself it's a daily trip to the mental gym. And no book of mine has been more fun in the making.

I chose my favorites and left out the random ones that stepped off the campaign trail. Actual headlines and my personal footnotes were added for context and to put the reader on the right bus to Crazytown.

P.S. I am very fond of the Republicans who buy my novels, and I hope one day to win back their votes.

June 27, 2011

Though only June, they've run for years.
They'll be disgraced & in arrears.
I'm here to parse the candidates
& be your wingman at debates.

"Waterloo Greets Hometown Girl"

—*Dallas Morning News*

June 27

Michele is 1st; hat's in the ring,
A darling of the far right wing.
If nothing else, a snappy dresser
& foster mom to scores, God bless 'er.

June 29

Michele is NOT a flake, Chris Wallace!
God's endorsement—plenty solace.
The nerve you had* re her IQ.
She went to Oral Roberts U!

*Bachmann to Wallace: Apology not accepted.

★

"Gingrich Found between Greece and Turkey"

—*Politico*

June 30

Where is Newt? I miss the strife,
His shrunken staff, his hungry* wife.
Inflame & chafe! Stay in the race!
It's only up from dead-last place.

*"'It's all about [Callista]. They do these movies together, and she does a word count: she has to have the same number of words on camera as he does or they have to reshoot.'"—Ariel Levy, *New Yorker*

"Palin: Paul Revere Warned the British"

—*LA Times*

July 4

To Founding Fathers we say thanks,
Lay flowers on their graves,
Like Paul Revere & Aaron Burr
(I *think* they freed the slaves).

☆

July 4 Extra

Thank Franklin Pierce & FDR,
John Hancock, Haley Barbour.
They rode to Concord, muskets high,
And dumped tea in the harbor.

"Bristol Palin: Bachmann Dresses a Lot Like My Mom, Doesn't She . . . ?"

—*NY Daily News*

July 5

Now Bachmann has her own loud bus.
The problem: "Whose is which?"
Will Palin think, "Homage on wheels"?
Or "Leave the trail, you bitch"?

☆

"Bachmann and Santorum Spark Furor over Slavery, 'Family Values'"

—Digg.com

July 9

Michele has signed a Values Pledge
Where sinning gets the boot.
You can't divorce, or lie, or cheat.
. . . Embarrassing for Newt.*

*He'd had an affair with Callista for six years before divorcing his second wife, Marianne, and had had an affair with Marianne while married to wife no. 1, Jacqueline Battley, the mother of his two actively campaigning daughters.

"Marcus Bachmann's Big Gay Mess"

—Gawker.com

July 13

Marcus Bachmann runs a clinic.
Helps you pray away the gay.
Feeling urges? Go to churches.
Find a clueless fiancée.

July 21

Michele we hear is prone to migraines.
So what's the giant ballyhoo?
Flesh to flesh with Mr. Bachmann,
I might get a headache, too.

"Rep. Giffords Makes Surprise Return to House Floor to Vote on Debt Ceiling"

—NY Daily News

Aug. 1

The vote was passed & it's been ugly.

Rogues or heroes? Can't discern.

Name a better civics lesson

Than Gabby Giffords' brave return?*

*Seven months after being shot in the head by an assailant in Tucson, Arizona.

Aug. 5

Meant to mention plunge in market,*

But found a nugget to impart:

Palin's eyesight fixed by Lasik.

Wears the glasses to look smart.

*More than 500 points.

"US Credit Rating Downgraded; 1st Time in History"

—*NY Post*

Aug. 6

Who needed this: a 2A rating,
Now the talk of every town.
Thanks, S & P, you S.O.B.s—
You kicked our guy when he was down.

★

"Perry Invites Massive Crowd to Pray for the Economy"

—YouTube

Aug. 7

Gov'ner Perry held a rally,
"Come to Pray" on letterhead!
Church & state? Why separate?
That's for Commies, Far Right said.

"Palin Takes Her Bus to Iowa; Oh, Look: It's the Ames Straw Poll"

—*LA Times*

Aug. 12

Palin's bus is on the way,
To Ames! So unrehearsed!
Limelight's great in any state,
Where rivals got there first.

★

"Texas Gov. Perry Makes Presidential Bid to End 'Rudderless Leadership'"

—Bloomberg.com

Aug. 13

"Windswept prairies" & the like,
Those pearls fill Perry's speech.
Many nods to faith & God.
To run, perchance to preach?

Aug. 14

Tim Pawlenty had no sizzle,
Dream is gone & money too.
Farewell . . . but wait! You're VP bait.*
Bland is good at number two.

*A contender? Nine months later, GOP insiders report that presumptive nominee Romney is looking for "a boring white guy" for his running mate.

Aug. 17

Perry hints our fighting force
May not respect Obama.
I'll make a bet troops won't forget
What happened to Osama.

Aug. 18

Michele has said on CNN:
I promise if elected,
Your gas will drop! 2 bucks a pop!
(No econ. course detected.)

★

Aug. 20

Global warming is a hoax,
And Darwin needs review.
The GOP is science-free,
And God loves CO_2.

Aug. 25

Here's a list of those not running:
Christie, Ryan, Palin, Jeb.
& where the hell went Bobby Jindal?
Too brown to be Tea-wing celeb?

⭐

"'His Crush on Me Was Weird and Creepy'"

—CNN.com

Aug. 26

El-Qaddafi has a crush,
On Condoleezza Rice!
The proof* was found in his compound
But Condi says, "No dice."

*A stash of photos of the American secretary of state. In a 2007 interview with Al Jazeera, Qaddafi described Rice as his "darling black African woman" and said, "I love her very much."

"East Coast Grids for Worst as Hurricane Irene Nears"

—NPR.org

Aug. 27

Let's not buy* Dick Cheney's memoir,
Mean VP & snarky crank.
Perhaps Irene will intervene,
& make his book tour tank.

*One should never discourage potential readers from purchasing books, even ones by war criminals.

☆

"Media, Politicians Hyping Hurricane to Push New Economic Restrictions"

—AmericanTradition.org

Aug. 28

Bachmann hates the EPA,
& FEMA bugs Ron Paul.
Kill Weather Service? Now I'm nervous.
Must I move to Montreal?

"Bachmann Sees Hurricane as Divine Message on Spending"

—Washington Monthly

Aug. 29

God is mad at Washington;
The weather makes that plain.
Bachmann says if she is prez,
We won't get hurricanes.

☆

"No. 1 Gov. in Executions: Rick Perry: 234 in 11 Years"

—Newser.com

Aug. 30

Perry's way ahead of Mitt,
In every Gallup poll.
If not his hair or frequent prayer,
Perhaps his death-row toll?

"'Jewish' Bachmann Is Costing Romney"

—NY Post

Sept. 2

Favorite story of this cycle:
Bachmann taken for a Jew.
It's a trick, sir: she's a shiksa.*
Ask at Oral Roberts U.

*Further hurting her Jewish cred was her pronouncing "chutzpah" as "choot-spa" on Fox News.

☆

"Mitt Romney Fights to Secure New Hampshire as Gingrich Surges"

—LA Times

Sept. 7

Mitt in shirtsleeves spoke in Concord,
Left in gleaming SUV.
No Q & A; just rushed away.
Not that cluster's cup of tea.

Sept. 8

Brian Williams said to Perry,
"100s killed on your death row."
That noble cause earned wild applause!*
And set Republicans aglow.

*"What do you make of that dynamic that just happened here?
The mention of the execution of 234 people drew applause?"
NBC's Williams asked as a follow-up. "I think Americans
understand justice," Perry replied.

☆

"Obama as Truman: 'Give 'em hell, Barry'?"

—*Roll Call*

Sept. 9

"Pass it now!" he scolded Congress,
Barack is back and on his game.
His plan was mapped & both sides clapped.
It's Harry Truman, press proclaims.

Sept. 10

Terror threat in New York City,
Coincides with Fashion Week.
Jihadist gang + Vera Wang.
Even when we're scared we're chic.

☆

Sept. 11

We praise the poetry of Jersey,
Not hallowed ground but standing by.
The chosen name for what it frames:
A monument called "Empty Sky."

Sept. 12

Today Pawlenty told reporters:
Romney is his favorite guy.
Somewhat boring?* Press ignoring?
They'd rather watch some paint go dry.

*Jon Stewart has referred to the ex-Minnesota governor as "Blanding J. Vanillaman."

☆

"Perry Gets Roughed Up in 2nd GOP Debate"

—*Texas Tribune*

Sept. 13

I love that Perry said so plainly,
"I can't be bought for just 5K."
So don't offend him! Best to send him,
A mil or two to pay & play.

"Tweet Your Meat, Lose Your Seat"

—t-shirt slogan

Sept. 14

Brooklyn, Queens, we hardly knew ye.
Jumped to GOP last night.
Because of Weiner, grass was greener?
Sexting* made you this uptight?

*It began the previous May when a photo of a man's crotch was uploaded to Weiner's Twitter account and soon it became apparent: not hacked.

☆

Sept. 20

Struck down today: Don't ask-Don't tell.
Good riddance, stupid ban!
One harsh upshot was troops less hot,
Less neat, less fun, less tan.*

*I worried that my stereotyping might offend, but my gay male Facebook friends went heavy on the "likes" that day.

"Cain Upsets Perry in Florida Straw Poll"

—Reuters

Sept. 25

The Sunshine State likes Herman Cain,
More than it likes Perry.
Thus pizza fans* have hurt some plans,
The party's worried? Verry.

*Cain took over the struggling chain Godfather's Pizza in 1986.
In *Politico*'s blind taste test, his samples got the booby prize. One
judge said, "It looked bad, it tasted bad, it just wasn't what you
want from a slice of pizza."

Sept. 27

Christie's saying, "I'm not ready,"
Despite what's sounding like a draft.
Too big to fail? He could prevail.
Think: Wm. Howard Taft.*

*At 332 pounds, "Big Bill" was the heaviest president (and also
the first to play golf). He liked milk so much that he brought his
own cow(s) to the White House.

Sept. 28

Let's remember late '07,
Giuliani led the pack.
The polls ordained he'd beat McCain,
While Clinton whipped Barack.*

*At this point, Cain is polling in first place; Rick Perry in second.

★

"GOP Crowd Abandons Patriotism for Bigotry"

—YouTube

Oct. 2

All candidates OK with boos,
For soldier who is gay.
They're fine with hate at each debate,
And then go home to pray.

"Is a Title and a Campaign Too WHAT?"

—*Language Log*

Oct. 6

Palin says the top job's "shackle-y."

So true: a bus tour is more fun.

Change-y, hopey, rogue-y, dopey

Maverick vocab 101*

*The *New Oxford American Dictionary* named Palin's "refudiate" the Word of the Year, an honor the Facebook term "unfriend" took home in 2010.

"84% Would Pay More under Cain's 9-9-9 Tax Plan"

—CNNMoney.com

Oct. 13

9-9-9! Annoy me not!

Already sick of Cain's lame plot.

His team forgot to share some facts.

New Hampshire, sir, has no sales tax.

Oct. 14

I Skyped with Herman Cain last night,
& asked if he'd be mine.*
A tad uptight, he didn't bite.
His answer? "Nein-Nein-Nein!"

*I posted this before his lady troubles began.

☆

"Cain Proposes Electrified Border Fence"
—*NY Times*

Oct. 17

Loaded guns, electric fences,
Or alligators in a moat.
"I'd give that order at the border."
It's Herman Cain I quote.

Oct. 20

Bachmann snagged a big endorsement!
Mr. Vegas! Yay, it's Wayne.
With lousy polls can this console?
A proud Michele says, "Danke Schoen."*

*Wayne Newton's first recording of his signature song was released
in 1963. In a news clip showing Newton endorsing and hugging
Michele, she wears a strained smile.

"Col. Qaddafi Killed: No Mercy for a Merciless Tyrant"

—*Telegraph* (UK)

Oct. 21

They're scared to utter a "well done"
When one more tyrant gets outrun.
"Most wanted" list is shrinking fast.
Yet GOP can't say congrats.

"Coming Soon to a Remainder Table Near You"

—Washington Post

Oct. 23

Going Rogue a half-price sale.
That happens when you leave the trail.
Walmart has a ton on hand.
Not big readers, Palin fans?

☆

Oct. 24

Rick Perry's bringing up again
The stalest false canard.
In a slump, you dine with Trump.
And play the Birther card.*

*Even though, six months before, President Obama released his long-form Hawaiian birth certificate, effectively silencing all but the obsessed. Almost immediately, Obama's campaign began selling birth-certificate t-shirts ($25) and mugs ($15). I own one of the latter.

Oct. 28

Obama's numbers creeping higher.
Not to say the guy's on fire,
But Dow is up; Qaddafi's dead,
& who wants Mitt in Lincoln's bed?

"Halloween Mask Sales May Predict Election"

—Kalamazoo Shopper

Oct. 29

I'm missing Palin in my verse,
Now trick-or-treaters make it worse.
Statistics show in costume shops,
This Halloween, her look's a flop.

"Herman Cain's Campaign Is Buying a Lot of Herman Cain Books"

—The Atlantic Wire

Oct. 30

You're still supporting Herman Cain?
This country's not a pizza chain!
Ex-staffers swear the guy's a schnook.
His business model: sell my book.

★

Oct. 31

O what a gift! The news is lewd.
2 female staffers have accused,
That frisky Cain of moves suggestive.
Romney's camp is downright festive.

Nov. 2

Cain's accuser soon will squawk,
Though contract says she cannot talk.
You know what's next: bring in the bride!
Show stoic wife at Herman's side.

☆

Nov. 3

Drip drip drip, a 3rd dame's out,
Confirming Cain is no Boy Scout.
The press's fault, his people claim:
It's race, not gropes, y'all should blame.

Nov. 7

I'm comin' 'round on Herman Cain,
Getting psyched for that campaign.
Against Barack in a debate?
Dear Networks: May I moderate?

☆

"Atty. Gloria Allred Enters Herman Cain Fray"

—Reuters

Nov. 8

Can you blame a guy for tryin'?
I grope & soon a lawyer's lyin'.
So sensitive! But where's her cred?
All I did was ask for head.

Nov. 9

What's a better bet on Cain,
Since sex has left its scars?
Will future be: the nominee,
Or *Dancing with the Stars*?

★

"OOPS; Rick Perry Can't Name 3 Agencies He'd Eliminate"

—*Fox News Insider*

Nov. 10

It's diagnosed: Rick P. is toast,
He famously went blank.
Who will reboot? The press says Newt,
That know-it-all & crank.

"All That Glitters May Redefine Run by Gingrich"

—NY Times

Nov. 12

Who's sitting pretty in the race?
It's Newt, who's now in 2d place.
He must believe that we forgot,
How many jewels Callista bought.*

*The former speaker acknowledged a second line of credit at
Tiffany and Co. for as much as $1 million, roughly a month
after personal financial-disclosure forms for Mrs. G. showed a
line of credit for between $250,000 and $500,000 there during
2005–2006.

★

Nov. 14

Green Bay tonight for Herman Cain,
Where football fans mix with campaign.
I cannot fail to take the bait:
He gives new meaning to "tailgate."

Nov. 15

Cain on Libya: Doesn't know
Where we stood & who's the foe.
Gaffe of gaffes! The worst oops yet.
Makes Perry seem an intellect.

★

"At $1.6 Million, Gingrich Is World's Highest-Paid Historian"

—*Christian Science Monitor*

Nov. 17

Dear Freddie Mac, it's me, your Newt,
I want to thank you for the loot.
Who knew that history could sell?
How come it isn't playing well?

Nov. 21

So Newt's on top & standing tall.
They love him & his Barbie doll.
But soon this blip will be reversed.
5 other flavors have known first.

★

"Scandal Makes Penn State a Fixture in Headlines"

—*NY Times*

Nov. 22

Debate tonight on CNN,
Must I sit thru this again?
Curse Obama! Voice your hate!
Next you'll blame him for Penn State.*

*An explosive sex-abuse scandal and possible cover-up rocked Pennsylvania State University and dominated the news for months after famed defensive coach Jerry Sandusky was arrested on Nov. 5.

Nov. 23

On CNN, at last nite's forum.
"Profile Muslims," said Santorum.
Ron Paul was quick to fire away:
"Can't terror look like Tim McVeigh?"

★

"Meghan McCain: 'Bachmann Is More Smarter Than Palin'"

—Townhall.com

Thanksgiving 2011

Today a trip down mem'ry lane,
In case Michele's been sounding sane
& charming on a late-nite show.
Debt-ceiling vote? A crazy No.

"Thanksgiving Greeting Reignites Culture Wars"

—DangerousIntersection.org

Nov. 26

So now we hear from zealot-cranks,
Who parsed Obama giving thanks.
The reason they're assigning blame?
He didn't mention God by name.

☆

"Gingrich Weaves Book, Movie Tour into Campaign"

—*Politico*

Nov. 27

Consultant this, consultant that,
His big head wears a dozen hats.
Milk every theme but kitchen sink
& run 4 prez as "Gingrich, Inc."

"For President, Newt Gingrich"

—Manchester Union Leader

Nov. 28

Big endorsement snagged by Newt,
Giving Mitt the front-page boot.
But who else did that paper flaunt?
Buchanan, Forbes, Pierre du Pont.

☆

"Barney Frank, Top Liberal, Won't Seek Re-election"*

—NY Times

Nov. 29

I serenade you, Barney Frank,
Brilliant wonk & witty crank.
You've had enuf. There's no good will.
But O what giant shoes to fill.

*The famously sweet Rep. Frank e-mailed me the same day my tweet appeared: "As a great Ogden Nash fan, I'm delighted to be the subject of a poem that evokes him to me."

Dec. 1

Professor Newt, he loves to teach,
For only 60K per speech.
When you are rich, you need not lobby.
Sell ideas, but call it "hobby."

☆

"Gingrich's Profound Insight on Poverty"
—Real clear Politics

Dec. 2

"Poor folks don't know how to work."
Who would say that but a jerk?
Adding insult, Newt implies,
Theft is how their kids get by.

"Defiant Herman Cain Suspends Campaign; Vows to Fight On"

—*LA Times*

Dec. 3

So many women felt his prod,
But Cain is now at peace with God.
Take your wife & go abroad,
Then mind the proverb, "Spare the rod."

☆

Dec. 4

Adultery fans, where can you turn
Now that Cain has crashed & burned?
Not Rick, not Mitt, not Dr. Paul.
That's right: Callista's butterball.

"Herman Cain's Presidential Campaign Is Bookended by the Theme to the Pokemon Movie"

—Village Voice

Dec. 5

We know that Cain's no Cicero,
He's not mistaken for Thoreau,
But when it's time to end his run,
Must his muse be Pokemon?

★

"Paying Homage to Trump's Towering Ego"

—Tampa Bay Times

Dec. 6

Newt & Donald sittin' in a tree,
K-I-S-S-I-N-G.
Sweet nothings must be loud & clear,
'Twixt blowhard couple of the year.

"Birther Donald Trump to Moderate Own Debate"

TheModerateVoice.com

Dec. 7

Late-night comics on TV
Want to thank the GOP,
Which said, "Let's run our own debate
& find an ass to moderate."

★

Dec. 8

Newt's way ahead in every state.
So who will be his running mate?
For balance, no one sharp or rich.
I'm thinking Rod Blagojevich.

Dec. 9

With Iowa a month away
What's on tap for Newt today?
At a store to pimp the mission:
Sell copies of the new edition.

☆

Dec. 11

A big exchange at 12th debate
On who's been faithful to their mates.
5 mentioned vows, then looked at Newt—
For once his bio left him mute.

"Big Barnstorm: Rick Perry on Two-Week Bus Tour in Iowa"

—*Des Moines Register*

Dec. 12

Perry plans a massive tour
To cities—count 'em—44.
His team would like his bus to hit
All who find gay rights legit.

✩

Dec. 14

I'm so depressed: no Trump debate.*
I'd cancelled work & saved the date.
At least there's hope: an indie run
By dimwit Birthers' favorite son.

*Only Gingrich and Santorum were going to show up. Trump's press release said, "The Republican Party candidates are very concerned that sometime after the final episode of *The Apprentice*, on May 20th, when the equal time provisions are no longer applicable to me, I will announce my candidacy for President of the United States."

Dec. 15

Mrs. Romney and her mate
Gave details of their hot first date:
That dev'lish Mitt! It sounds so right:
'Twas *Sound of Music* that big night.

☆

"Callista Gingrich: Author, French Horn Play, Choir Singer"

—Newt2012.org

Dec. 17

This weekend Newt will not campaign.
Instead on tour down Lovers' Lane.
As prez, I'd fear a hen-pecked mister,
Who'd pledge allegiance to Callista.

Dec. 19

In Iowa it's all reversed,
Ron Paul has taken over 1st.
Air's leaking out of Newt's balloon.
Farewell, late surge! You came too soon.

⭐

"Gingrich Continues His Crusade against Activist Judges"

—*NY Times*

Dec. 20

Scary crazy stupid stance:
Subpoena judges,* make them dance.
Ignore decisions you don't like?
Welcome to the Gingrich Reich.

*And how would he get these judges to testify? He'd send the Capitol Police or U.S. marshals to subpoena any federal judge who issued an opinion "out of sync with American values." Then, as Gingrich said on *Face the Nation* on Dec. 17, he'd have Congress impeach the judge.

Dec. 21

What gives the GOP elation?
A presidential long vacation.
But now their taunt is overblown:
Michelle & daughters went alone.

☆

"Gingrich in Iowa: Big Money and Negative Ads Are Crushing Him"

—Slate

Dec. 22

Attack ads boosting Dr. Paul,
Now Gingrich is above it all.
Too statesmanlike to vent his spleen?
But buddy, you invented "mean."

"Romney Could 'Convince' Christie to Run for VP"

—*Philadelphia Inquirer*

Dec. 24

Despite the loud NO voiced before,
Christie didn't close the door.
If Romney had to balance "nice,"
A gasbag might be good as vice.

★

Dec. 25

To scratch the presidential itch,
Trump has made a party switch.
Now independent & rewired,
Translation: "GOP, you're fired!"

"Gingrich Accepting Gore Invite Lands on Loveseat with Pelosi"

—Bloomberg.com

Dec. 26

In Iowa they hate Pelosi;
That ad, on couch? He looked too cozy.
Newt takes it back & reassures:
Cooperation nevermore!

☆

Dec. 28

The Gingrich cry: "Let's set a date!
A Lincoln-Douglas-style debate!*
90 minutes, to the wall!"
Convinced he'll beat the pants off all.

*"The *American Spectator*'s Quin Hillyer calls it 'the fallacy of the master debater'—the belief that elections turn on dramatic rhetorical confrontations, in which the smarter and better-spoken candidate exposes his rival as a tongue-tied boob." —*NY Times*, Dec. 10, 2011

Dec. 29

For Gingrich not a happy phase:
Down 20 points in 20 days.
How to handle such a wobble?
Better buy the wife a bauble.

☆

"Bachmann's Iowa Chair Jumps Ship"

—New York

Dec. 30

Heard that Bachmann's guy defected,
Sure she'd never be elected.
He should adjust his crystal ball
If White House shingle says, "Ron Paul."

Dec. 31

It surely hasn't been mundane,
The year that gave us Herman Cain.
As I stroll down memory lane,
I miss his mistressy campaign.

☆

Jan. 1, 2012

Monotony! It's gaining ground!
And faithful Mitt won't screw around.
A Saint of Latter Day persuasion,
He's proud to be a dry Caucasian.

"With Just 2 Days Left, Santorum Has the Hot Hand"

—*Des Moines Register*

Jan. 2

Will Rick Santorum be the guy?
Loves babies, God & apple pie.
In single digits once, but still
In sweater vest he's dressed to kill.

☆

Jan. 3

Rick & Paul & Newt & Mitt!
Who will win & who might quit?
It's caucus day & we're all braced
To see who pleases all-white taste.

"Santorum: I Might Win Iowa Caucuses Recount"

—Politico

Jan. 4

The newest sweetheart of the Right,
Santorum had a red-hot night.
Romney won, but 'twas a squeaker.
& down in 4th, a pissed-off speaker.

⭐

Jan. 4 Extra

The time has come to say farewell,
To mega–foster mom Michele.
She prays to God her soul to keep,
& while He's at it, make her veep.

"Finished Assessing, Perry Ready to Dive Back In"

—*The Atlantic*

Jan. 5

"A little prayer & some reflection,"
Meaning, "Adios, election."
So we *thought.* But Perry's back.
That's 1 flip-flop he won't attack.

☆

Jan. 6

Mitt endorsed by John McCain,
Excitement builds in that campaign.
Is that not true? No voters cared?
They're waiting for the undeclared.

"Same-Sex Marriage Follows Santorum around New Hampshire"

—Huffington Post

Jan. 7

Gay weddings, not his cuppa tea
(Santorum fears polygamy).
Could NO on same-sex marriage screw him?
College students roundly boo him.

☆

"Republicans Pound Each Other in Debate"

—Dallas Morning News

Jan. 9

Baloney of the pious type!
—Most quoted anti-Romney swipe.
Keep it up and shoot your wad,
Form the circular firing squad.*

*Gingrich *used* to quote what he called Ronald Reagan's 11th
Commandment—Thou shall not speak ill of fellow Republicans.

Jan. 10

Today the Granite Staters vote,
& how they love to rock the boat!
Known to humble & surprise,
2d place can seem the prize.

☆

"No Surprise*: Romney Runs Away with It in New Hampshire"*

—Yahoo.com

Jan. 11

Romney wins—not unexpected.
Perry's numbers? Undetected.
And next for Newt, the biggest mouth?
Oh, yes, indeed: he's going south.

*Except for the *Boston Globe*'s endorsement of Jon Huntsman.

Jan. 12

Have you noticed favorite diss?
It's "European Socialist!"
Cuts Obama down to size?
Or just recalls those "freedom fries"?

⭐

Jan. 13

Newt's latest ad attacking Mitt
Exposes why the guy's unfit:
Besides the sins of Bain finance
The traitor speaks *la langue de France.**

*Loudly *not* anti-intellectual, Gingrich declared in 1995, "I am the most seriously professorial politician since Woodrow Wilson."

Jan. 14

Again! The famous Perry flub
(What departments would he scrub?).
"3 off the bat . . ." he starts to say
And lives to goof another day.

⭐

"Are You There, God? It's Me, Tim Tebow"
—WickedGoodSports.com

Jan. 15

God had better things to do
Than guide the ball that Tebow threw.
With people sick & starved & maimed,
You think He watches Bronco games?*

*This had nothing to do with any campaign. In political parlance,
it was an outlier tweet.

Jan. 16

Huntsman's getting out today.
The Far Right found him D.O.A.
His Mandarin* was wearing thin
Nor does he hate enough to win.

*Joe Scarborough compared Huntsman's use of Mandarin to Mitt Romney's gaffe when he said he liked to fire people: "You don't speak Mandarin during a Republican debate!"

"Newt Gingrich Shows Why He Is Unelectable"

—*Telegraph* (UK)

Jan. 17

The audience was loving Newt.
They found his racist quips so cute.
"Food Stamp Prez!" That really played
As bigotry was on parade.

Jan. 19

Newt's Marianne, the 2nd wife,
Presumably will twist the knife.
Tonight on air she might unveil
Some juicy stuff that could derail.

★

Jan. 20

Ex-Mrs. G., you told the truth,
Open marriage *is* uncouth.
Newt promised love; he swooned & kissed ya,
Then left you for the loose Callista.

"Mitt Romney Sings 'America the Beautiful,' Awkwardness Ensues ..."

—TheHollywoodGossip.com

Jan. 20 extra

The voice, alas, was Red State white,

The patriotic hymn not right.

As Romney butchered sing-along,

Obama killed with Al Green song.*

*The same week Obama brought down the house with "Let's Stay Together" at the Apollo, Romney was compelled to sing "America the Beautiful" at every event.

★

"As S.C. Primary Dawns, Can Romney Keep Gingrich at Bay?"

—CBSNews.com

Jan. 21

Did Newt's eruption hit the spot?

Is Bain a dog that bit or not?

Will tax forms be the acid test?

Or will it be the sweater vest?*

*On Jan. 9, *Time* named Santorum's vests no. 1 on its list of "Top 10 Political Fashion Statements."

"Gingrich Resurrects Campaign, Scrambles Race with S.C. Win"

—Fox News

Jan. 22

Newt mocked & railed & condescended
Now the race has been upended.
It all came down to 1 debate,
& Carolina bought the hate.

☆

"Florida Debate: Where's the Love?"

—*Christian Science Monitor*

Jan. 24

When audience is held to mute,
We get a paler shade of Newt.
Without the precious boos and cheers,
Sound bites miss that special sneer.

Jan. 26

Newt is big in outer space,
Wants to build a lunar base.*
And flights to Mars! Another pledge
(In case you doubt he's on the edge).

*This was a wonderful gift to political satirists, second only to his serial divorces.

★

"The Jacksonville Brawl"

—RedState.com

Jan. 27

So very rich! Last nite's debate!
Wolf Blitzer came to moderate.
He fired back when Gingrich pounced,
Thus Romney's comeback was announced.

Jan. 28

We see from tax forms Romney files,
His dough is in the Cayman Isles
And Switzerland's obliging banks:
Mitt's bottom line sends grateful thanks.

☆

Jan. 29

Newt's the choice of Herman Cain.
Not quite a boost to his campaign.
The wives wore smiles that were polite,
While thinking, *Lover boys unite.*

Jan. 30

Oh it's nasty on the trail,
Newt is fighting tooth & nail.
"Moderate Massachusetts liar!"
No condemnation any higher!

☆

"Gingrich Robocall: Romney Forced Holocaust Survivors to Eat Non-Kosher Food"

—*Huffington Post*

Jan. 31

Pandering—thou name is Newt.
In Florida, will it bear fruit?
So obvious it does amuse:
"Mitt cut Kosher meals for Jews!"

"After Florida Loss, Gingrich Says He Still Expects to Be Nominee"

—CBSNews.com

Feb. 1

Newt ungracious in defeat,
Inauguration plans complete.
So positive he will succeed,
Forgot he lost & should concede.

⭐

"Trump Endorses Romney after Puzzling Vegas Day"

—*Newsday*

Feb. 3

Who will follow Trump's advice?
Voters who have trophy wives,
Birthers & *Apprentice* fans,
Republicans with golden tans.

Feb. 5

So clear that Romney couldn't lose,
Nevada caucus was a snooze.
His singing's bad; he can't amuse.
I got me the robot blues.

★

"Casino Mogul Sheldon Adelson's Family Bankrolling Gingrich"

—*Washington Post*

Feb. 6

Sheldon A., my PAC's for sale.
I'll never not back Israel.
My campaign coffers are in debt.
I'll put you in my cabinet.

Feb. 8

Farewell, Defense of Marriage Act!
Same-sex weddings back on track.
The institution is so nice
That politicians do it thrice.

☆

"Rational Irrationality: Santorum Sweep Stuns Mitt"

—*New Yorker*

Feb. 8

Just as Mitt could really bore 'em,
We get a sweep from Rick Santorum.
3 states* move to farther right.
God got thanked a lot last night.

*MN, MO, CO.

"I Was JFK's Teenage Mistress"

—CNN.com

Feb. 10

Now I've said it, come what may:
I also slept with JFK.
It took a lifetime to unveil,
But now my memoir is for sale.

☆

Feb. 11

Rick's trifecta* was a stunner,
But isn't Mitt your true frontrunner?
Someone tell him what to say,
Like "Dad was poor" & "Don't be gay."

*TN, OK, ND

"CPAC 2012: Sarah Palin, Motivator-in-Chief"*

—*Washington Post*

Feb. 12

Who is still their favorite pol?
Who's the fairest of them all?
Who thinks she is the nominee?
It's CPAC's darling, Sarah P.

*"Sarah Palin strode out on stage at the Conservative Political Action Conference in Washington carrying a red leather briefcase— and off to work she went, firing off a year's worth of sarcastic one-liners at 'Professor Obama'" —Melinda Henneberger

⭐

Feb. 14

Callista, please be mine forever.
When will I forsake you? Never!
Yes, I had a marriage spree,
But Valentine, it stops at 3.

"Finding Justice: The Unsettling Case of Seamus Romney"*

—LifewithDogs.tv

Feb. 15

Polls in Michigan no fun,

If you are Mitt, the native son.

Motor City's living proof

They hate when dogs ride on their roofs.

*Gail Collins, to my ongoing delight, finds a way to mention Seamus or his crate regularly in her *New York Times* column.

★

"Men, All Men. And Birth Control"

—*The Nation*

Feb. 17

A panel came to testify,

All were clergy; all were guys.

If contraception is the topic,

Might priests be just a tad myopic?

Feb. 18

Christie vetoes same-sex marriage.
Is this a value to disparage?
Is true love something to deplore
In state that gave us *Jersey Shore*?

★

"Romney Breaks Losing Streak, Wins Maine Caucuses"*

—MSNBC.com

Feb. 19

Is Gingrich going down the drain,
Despite the boost from Herman Cain?
I'd miss the mission to the moon
& hair that holds in a typhoon.**

*Newt finishes 4th, edging out "Other."

**"[Callista's] hair is platinum blond and very stiff, with one remarkable lock styled into an immobile, upward swoosh." —Ariel Levy, *New Yorker*

Feb. 20

Coded in his "vote for me,"
Santorum cites theology.
"Obama's different" is the claim.
"*Says* he's Christian"—that old game.

★

"Santorum: 'Birth Control Harms Women and Society'"

—DailyKos.com

Feb. 22

Welcome to the time machine,
Press "Santorum" on your screen,
Hit "vision for the family,"
Get "large & contraception-free."

"Newt, Happy Warrior"

—*Politico*

Feb. 23

Oh really, Newt? When asked to tell
1 word that sums you up quite well.
You answered "cheerful" with a smile.
You? The poster child for bile.

★

"Bailout Stand Trails Romney in Car Country"

—*NY Times*

Feb. 24

If Romney had his crystal ball out,
Mighta seen there'd be a fallout:
Use of "bankrupt"—sure to haunt him.
In 2012 Detroit won't want him.

Feb. 25

"4 cars & 2 are Cadillacs."
Proudly Mitt displays his knack
For underscoring in his pitch,
There's no escaping Richie Rich.

☆

Feb. 27

Mitt thinks that he shall never see
A poll as lovely as a tree.
Tho roundly teased & misconstrued,
His home state* has him up by two.

*MI, as opposed to those other home states: MA, NH, CA.

Feb. 28

NASCAR fan? Mitt nearly beams.
No, but wealthy friends own teams.
His filter clearly nonexistent,
A gaffe a day & so consistent!

★

Feb. 28 Extra

College is for snobs, Santorum?
Hard to hear the week of Purim.
I cannot speak for every Jew,
But education's helped a few.

"Catholic Vote Eludes Santorum in Michigan"

—*NY Times*

Feb. 29

Farewell to chaos once predicted.
It left with wounds Rick self-inflicted.*
Now Mitt has had a 2-state sweep,
And still it's putting us to sleep.

*On the eve of the primary, Santorum said Kennedy's 1960
speech on religion made him want to throw up. Two days later he
said he regretted the remark—or the blowback, perhaps.

⭐

"Mitt Romney Is Delighted to Go Hunting with You"

—YouTube

Mar. 1

Talkin' guns, Mitt isn't tame!
Rats & bunnies his big game.
In jeans, no jacket & no tie,
He's every inch the common guy.

Mar. 4

Rush rushes to apologize,
Admits his use of "slut" unwise.*
"Be like me & not so wanton:
Trade the Pill for Oxycontin."**

*"What does it say about the college co-ed Susan Fluke [*sic*; her name is Sandra], who goes before a congressional committee and essentially says that she must be paid to have sex. What does that make her? It makes her a slut, right? It makes her a prostitute. She wants to be paid to have sex. She's having so much sex she can't afford the contraception. She wants you and me and the taxpayers to pay her to have sex. … Okay, so she's not a slut. She's round-heeled." —*The Rush Limbaugh Show*, Feb. 29

**He was arrested in '06 on prescription-drug charges.

★

"Gingrich's Georgia Win Masks Southern State Strategy"

—Reuters

Mar. 5

Be prepared: It will be tough
Watching Gingrich strut his stuff.
Stay tuned to hear him bloviate
On narrow win in his home state.

Mar. 6

I dreamed that Limbaugh went to jail.
No advertisers paid his bail.
The judge said life without parole
& good luck there with birth control.

★

"Romney Takes 6 out of 10 Super Tuesday Contests"

—USA Today

Mar. 8

Back & forth, the two teams shout:
You get out, no YOU get out!
Newt tells Rick he'd sweep the Right.
Rick tells Newt: Go fly a kite.

"Romney's Grits & Catfish Act Goes Too Far"

—*Boston Herald*

Mar. 9

Advice down south for northern Mitt,
Be seen enjoying shrimp 'n' grits.
"Y'all" is good & NASCAR's great.
Healthcare's bad & sushi's bait.

☆

Mar. 10

Some territories have no qualm;
Mitt wins all delegates in Guam!
A distant isle in the Pacific,
From far away, he seems terrific.

Mar. 11

Kansas went for Rick Santorum.
They love his preacher-like decorum.
On the map the state is square:
A quality that wins big there.

★

Mar. 12

You must've heard the speculation,
The rumor now in circulation:
Perry runs with Newt this fall
Malaprop meets know-it-all.

"Mississippi, Alabama and the Power of Political Surprises"

—*Washington Post*

Mar. 14

Santorum had a 2-win night,
& not 1 pollster got it right.
Of course we get the Gingrich spin:
Brilliant Me is staying in.

☆

"Sarah Palin Not Embarrassed Enough This Week, Would Like to Debate Obama, Please"

—*Wonkette*

Mar. 15

Mrs. Palin, it's too late
To ask Obama to debate.
Game Change hurt; you sure looked mean.
Take heart: in Tea Land you're still queen.

Mar. 17

St. Paddy's Day: green will be worn,
No matter who is native born.
Santorum might think twice today
Before he disses JFK.

★

"Crowd Horrified When 2 Dudes Kiss"

—Gawker.com

Mar. 18

It wasn't up Santorum's alley,
2 men smooching at his rally.
You've made your point, now go away.
Only Democrats are gay.

Mar. 19

Puerto Rico's vote unsplit:
All delegates signed on for Mitt.
Must not've mentioned in San Juan,
"Your gifted people cut my lawn."

★

Mar. 20

Dad of seven? Dad of five?
One prays on stage; one loves to drive.
Dog-on-Roof or Altar Boy?
Who will win in Illinois?

"Romney's Big Day Marred by Etch-a-Sketch Remark"

—CNN.com

Mar. 22

Mitt gets the blessing of Jeb Bush,
& then a swift kick to the tush.
The Etch-a-Sketch: foes' instant prop,
A synonym for "He flip-flops."

★

"Newt's Hopes Dashed in Alabama, Mississippi"

—*Huffington Post*

Mar. 25

If spying on the Gingrich camp,
Would we see an exit ramp?
Does ANY outcome cause self-doubt?
Can Newt pronounce, "I should get out"?

Mar. 27, R.I.P. Trayvon Martin

"A son of mine would look like that,"
& Gingrich takes it to the mat.
"Appalling!" does not fit the bill,
for crime evoking Emmett Till.

☆

Mar. 29

Pose with Gingrich & his bride!
A souvenir pre-Newticide:
For 50 bucks a photo op,
Quick before he closes shop.

Mar. 30

It's been confirmed: a secret meet.
In New Orleans, a hotel suite.
Newt & Romney 'round a table.
There's a ticket: Cain & Abel.

★

"Romney Home Is Mitt for a King"

—*NY Daily News*

Mar. 31

I need a lift for all my cars,
My Cadillacs & sleek Jaguars.
It's so unfair, this condemnation
About a beach-house renovation.

Apr. 3

I'm watching Palin on *Today*,
Her rhinestone flag pin on display.
Perhaps while on the morning team,
U shouldn't call your host lamestream.

★

"Romney Sweeping Up Delegates"

—ThePoliticalZealot.com

Apr. 4

Presumptive ho-hum nominee,
Mitt Romney captured 3 of 3.*
Farewell, good times & here comes Bain.
I sure miss Bachmann, Newt & Cain.

*DC, MD, WI.

"Republican Endorsement[s] of Romney Remain Tepid"

—Salt Lake Tribune

Apr. 5

Tho all sewed up & Tampa looms,
There's worry in the smoke-filled rooms.
Endorsements fill the air 4 Mitt,
Yet every one sounds counterfeit.

★

"Golfer-in-Chief to Augusta: 'Let Those Women Play!'"

—Yahoo Sports

Apr. 6

The jobless rate at 4-year low,
The Right will make a tale of woe.
"The deficit! The price of gas!
& keep dames off Augusta's grass!"

Apr. 8

On Easter Sunday one might ask:
About an uphill campaign task.
The Right expects it will get slammed.
Is Mitt the sacrificial lamb?

★

"FINALLY? Newt Might Drop Out If He Doesn't Win Delaware"

—*Business Insider*

Apr. 9

Sinking Gingrich still won't qult,
His mission only: torment Mitt.
He claims the urge to reassess
Is purely in the heads of press.

"Gingrich Says Campaign 'On a Shoestring'"

—FoxNews.com

Apr. 10

"Glad I did this; no regrets."
"& yes we have amassed some debts."
Is this a note of common sense:
At last Newt's using the past tense.

★

"'There are currently no events scheduled. Check back frequently for updated announcements.'"

—RickSantorum.org

Apr. 11

Sayonara, Rick Santorum.
Your kids, we know, you do adore 'em.
We'll miss your angry, preachy quotes,
& Mitt says thanks for home state votes.

Apr. 12

It isn't fair! The untrue rap:
That Romney has a gender gap!
He'll fight for jobs for laid-off ladies.
He wants our mutts atop Mercedes.

⭐

"Hilary Rosen Apologizes to Ann Romney, Calls for End to 'Faux War' against Moms"

—Huffington Post

Apr. 13

Grab that stay-at-home-mom thing.
Pretend it spoke for whole left wing.
Ann is great, star of the show.
But Romney still has women's woes.

Apr. 14

Romney speaks to NRA
To reassure them he's OK
With guns of every make & size
& campus nuts who terrorize.

☆

"Dick Cheney Recovering after Getting a New Heart"

—*NY Times*

Apr. 16

3 weeks after operation
Cheney's growling to the nation.
No transplant & no angioplasty
Makes a sullen veep less nasty.

Apr. 17

Bit by penguin at the zoo,
What's a candidate to do?
Soon the bird wrote in his blog,
"Newt tastes like an underdog."

★

"Cain on Gingrich: 'I Don't Know What's Going On in His Head'"

—DailyCaller.com

Apr. 18

Et tu, Herman, my old friend,
Saying that my run must end.
Callista's mad you broke our date
To donors' night, 5 bucks a plate.

"Happy Birthday, Ann Lois Romney"

—ChicagoNow.com

Apr. 19

Your spouse is all but nominated,
A million rich jokes circulated.
Did no one think it was foolhardy
To let The Donald host your party?

★

"Romney Sparks Outrage in Pittsburgh"

—Inquisitr.com

Apr. 20

Insult a baker? Cookiegate!
Small diss? Or does it demonstrate
That Mitt not only can't relate,
But could screw up with heads of state?

"Americanos Behaving Badly"

—*NY Daily News*

Apr. 21

Si, Secret Service compromised
& now it's been politicized.
Palin, in a Fox News clip,
Blamed the prez for what's unzipped.

★

"Romney Visits Closed Factory to Mock Obama"

—*Wall Street Journal*

Apr. 22

Once again, it's Mitt's tin ear
At warehouse closed in George Bush years.
Obama blamed; that's how it's spun.
Awkward optics 101.

Apr. 23

Newt, you're costing us too much.
Can't your PAC at least go Dutch?
For Secret Service every day
Our taxes shell out $40K.

★

"Romney, Rubio Mum on Vice Presidential Prospects"

—TeaParty.org

Apr. 24

¡Hola, it's Rubio & Mitt!
On the stump & so close-knit.
Polls have NOT induced a panic,
But please note that my pal's Hispanic.

Apr. 25

Who knows how to underwhelm?
Who's sitting pretty at the helm?
It's Romney after five dull wins.
For Newt: let's cue the violins.

★

Apr. 26

Reasons for my Gingrich blues:
No lunar dreams or Grecian cruise,
No credit line from Tiffany's,
No saintly wife, his former squeeze.

Apr. 27

Newt's a sport! He'll stump for Mitt.
Might grouches mutter "hypocrite"?
You flop & when you're in retreat,
You've got a lotta words to eat.

✩

"Gingrich Announces That He Will Announce His Exit"

—*NY Times*

Apr. 28

Why so long? Why wait 'til Tuesday?*
Was he planning 1 last squeeze play?
Now we know, and lord, it's true,
Agenda stated: Visit zoo.

*"Most losing presidential candidates want to slink away, unnoticed, with brief statements that their campaign has run its course. Not Newt Gingrich." —Michael D. Shear, *NY Times*, May 1, 2012

Apr. 29

Mitt must wait to get his bounce,
Now Newt says Wednesday he'll announce.
Extension, please; he needs a day
Before he PACs his dream away.

⭐

Apr. 30

White House Correspondents' Dinner,
A lotta laffs; Barack a winner.
Vote presidential comedy
& spare us Mitt's delivery.

GOP's Silly Slam of President Obama for 'Spiking the Ball'"

—LA Times

May 1

It's a fact: Osama's dead,
A feat that makes the Right see red.
What's to scorn about that raid?
It showed Obama unafraid.

May 2

Farewell to Newt & current Mrs.!
But wait, his verb choice is suspicious.
"Suspend" in lieu of "Now I quit"?
Also missing: "Vote for Mitt."

May 3

A brief good-bye; well, brief for Newt,
It took a while to self-salute
His brain, his aims, his derring-do,
All coming soon to town near you.

May 4

Michele's on board, endorsing Mitt!
She grinned & waved & picked no nits.
Just showing up: does that win votes?
I'd better put "endorse" in quotes.

May 5

Romney & Santorum met,
So was it all forgive-forget?
Tho no one left a bloody corpse,
The fight was called before "endorse."

☆

May 7

Joe Biden's message went off-track,
& White House had to walk him back:
Gay marriage? He's on board with that.
Let's hear it in a Fireside Chat.

May 8

Santorum in the dark of night
At last gave Mitt a dim green light.
Consensus is he could do better,
Than 13th graf of mousy letter.

★

May 9

Adieu last moderate Richard Lugar,
A toast with champagne & beluga.
T-party didn't like your style:
They hate that reach across the aisle.

May 10

A landmark day! A joy to tweet,
His evolution is complete.
Go forth & wed! All "I do's" equal!
Don't ask-Don't tell gets gutsy sequel.

May 15

Ron Paul acknowledged he can't win,
Tho we'd forgotten he was in.
Some say it's wise to abdicate
When you don't carry any state.

May 17

Underwhelming, mildly pleasant,
OK it wasn't effervescent,
With elevator button pushed,
"I'm for Romney," sighed George Bush.

☆

May 26

Like Clooney's bash,* but it's for Mitt,
Host Trump is back to Birther shit.
Don't just say, "His view's not mine";
Denounce it like you have a spine.

*An A-list party on May 10 at George Clooney's house raised a reported $15 million for the president, who made his way to all 14 tables.

June 6

Bye-bye Paycheck Fairness Act,
The ladies once again get smacked.
The GOP all voted nay,
Good luck, you guys, election day.

★

June 10

A theory getting wide attention
Is sabotage of job creation.
Republicans' election goal:
Economy in toilet bowl.

June 16

Immigration overhaul:
Young migrants feeling 10 ft. tall.
Obama said, "You're not to blame
If just a kid when parents came."

June 18

Romney's bus is painted quaint;
Its symbols won't bring 1 complaint:
Silos! Lighthouse! Art naive.
It's 1950s Mittbelieve.

☆

June 28

SCOTUS broke its recent mold,
Handing down a nice uphold!
Meanwhile back in Romney camp
Handkerchiefs & brows are damp.

Elinor Lipman is the author of nine novels, including *The Family Man*, *The Inn at Lake Devine*, and *Then She Found Me*, which was adapted into a 2008 feature film. Her essays have appeared in the *New York Times*'s "Modern Love" and "Writers on Writing" columns, and in the *Boston Globe* and *Washington Post*. Her next novel, *The View from Penthouse B*, and an essay collection, *I Can't Complain*, will be published in May 2013. She held the 2011–2012 Elizabeth Drew Chair in Creative Writing at Smith College.

Continue to follow Elinor Lipman's election-season tweets . . .

On Twitter: @ElinorLipman
On Facebook: facebook.com/elinor.lipman